MovieGen AI

Meta's Game-Changer in Visual Storytelling

Explore the Future of Filmmaking, Text-to-Video, and Dynamic Editing

Kylan P.crook

TABLE OF CONTENT

INTRODUCTION

In recent years, artificial intelligence has reshaped countless industries, but few transformations have been as captivating as the rise of AI in filmmaking. The art of storytelling through visual media has always demanded an intricate balance of creativity, technology, and imagination. Now, AI has entered this space, not as a passive tool but as a game-changer, altering the very foundation of how visual content is produced. Picture a world where the creation of cinematic magic, once the domain of a select few, is now within reach of anyone with a vision and a text prompt. This is the dawn of a new era in filmmaking, and Meta's MovieGen AI stands at its forefront.

The rapid evolution of AI technologies has pushed boundaries that once seemed insurmountable. From simple image recognition models to complex systems capable of generating lifelike visuals, the journey of AI has been nothing short of astonishing. Yet, when it comes to visual content creation, the stakes are higher. We're talking about reproducing the nuanced details that define reality—lighting, physics, reflections, and even the intangible atmosphere of a scene. Meta, a company known for its bold ventures into new tech frontiers, has taken a surprising leap into this space. When most expected them to focus on social media and virtual spaces, they quietly developed one of the most powerful AI-driven video creation systems we've seen to date: MovieGen.

At first glance, Meta's entry into the video AI realm might seem unexpected. After all, there are companies that have spent years perfecting video-generating AI models. But Meta's quiet, calculated move into this space was more than just an expansion of their AI portfolio—it was a statement. MovieGen was developed to do more than just follow in the footsteps of its predecessors. It was designed to redefine the standard. In a world where content is king, Meta has given creators the ultimate key to unlock a new dimension of video creation. Imagine being able to describe a scene—no cameras, no actors, no location scouting—and watch as that vision materializes on screen with stunning accuracy. This isn't science fiction anymore; this is MovieGen.

So, what makes MovieGen so special? For starters, it's powered by a staggering 30 billion parameter model, a scale that puts it leagues ahead of many existing video AI systems. It's not just about generating images or short clips; MovieGen can create full-fledged, coherent videos from a simple text prompt. And the results are nothing short of breathtaking. Visuals that would normally require entire teams of skilled professionals can now be produced with just a few lines of input.

It's like having a director, a cinematographer, and a special effects team all rolled into one AI-driven powerhouse.

But it's not just about generating visuals. MovieGen also comes equipped with a 13 billion parameter model for sound, seamlessly pairing audio with the video it creates. Think of the possibilities: not only can you generate a beautiful scene, but you can also add immersive soundscapes, perfectly timed music, and authentic sound effects, all automatically. The level of detail and precision is unmatched, making the entire process of content creation faster, smoother, and infinitely more accessible.

As Meta introduces this revolutionary tool, it's hard not to feel a sense of awe. The sheer potential of MovieGen is staggering. For filmmakers, content creators, marketers, and artists alike, this is more than just another AI tool—it's a portal into the future of visual storytelling. The platform has outperformed competitors like Runway Gen 3 and Sora, systems that were once considered the pinnacle of video AI technology. By stepping into the arena, Meta hasn't just kept pace with industry leaders; they've surpassed them in several key areas, from the realism of the generated physics to the lifelike quality of the lighting.

Meta's move into video AI with MovieGen is a signal that the future of visual storytelling is being rewritten. And it's not just about making content creation easier; it's about enhancing creativity in ways we've never seen before. Suddenly, the only limit is the storyteller's imagination. MovieGen takes care of the rest, rendering scenes with precision and beauty, breathing life into ideas that were once confined to the mind.

This introduction is just the tip of the iceberg. MovieGen AI promises to revolutionize not only how we create visual content but also how we think about creativity itself. Meta's foray into this field marks the beginning of a new chapter for both AI and filmmaking, one where the possibilities are truly limitless. And as we turn the page, the excitement only grows, with each revelation about this groundbreaking technology offering another reason to believe that the future of filmmaking has arrived.

Chapter 1: A New Era in Video Creation

The world of video creation has always been driven by a quest for better visuals, more realistic scenes, and the seamless blending of imagination and reality. Traditionally, filmmakers relied on massive teams of experts to bring their visions to life, spending countless hours on every detail, from set design to post-production. But with the introduction of AI, the rules of the game are changing. At the center of this transformation is Meta's MovieGen, a technological marvel that has redefined what is possible in video generation.

The breakthrough of MovieGen lies in its 30 billion parameter model, a scale so vast that it sets a new standard for AI-driven video creation. For context, parameters are the internal elements of an AI model that allow it to process and learn from data. The more parameters, the more sophisticated the model becomes, enabling it to understand and replicate complex tasks with remarkable precision. MovieGen's 30 billion parameters put it ahead of its time, allowing it to generate not just simple images but entire video sequences from text prompts. This scale is unprecedented, giving Meta a distinct edge over its competitors.

One of the most remarkable aspects of MovieGen is how it manages to outperform established players in the video AI field, such as Runway Gen 3 and Sora. These systems were considered cutting-edge until MovieGen arrived. Runway Gen 3 had been praised for its ability to create dynamic video from text, while Sora impressed with its intricate visuals and smooth animations. However, MovieGen has raised the bar by delivering visuals that are more immersive, more lifelike, and, most importantly, more accessible to creators at all levels.

The quality and detail of the content it produces have caught the AI community off guard, surpassing even the most optimistic predictions.

What sets MovieGen apart isn't just the number of parameters it utilizes but how those parameters are applied to key elements of visual storytelling. At the heart of any great video lies the mastery of lighting and physics. These two factors are notoriously difficult for AI models to handle, often resulting in uncanny or flat-looking visuals. In many AI-generated videos, lighting either fails to interact correctly with objects or doesn't reflect natural conditions, leaving scenes looking artificial. MovieGen, however, has found a way to bring real-world lighting dynamics into its generated videos.

Lighting is not just about brightness or darkness; it's about how light interacts with different materials, how shadows shift as the sun moves, and how reflections play across surfaces. MovieGen understands this nuance, offering a level of sophistication that mimics the subtlety of natural lighting. Whether it's the reflection of sunlight on water or the way shadows move across a character's face, MovieGen gets it right. The result is a video that feels real, that draws viewers in with its authenticity, even when the content is completely AI-generated.

Physics is another area where MovieGen excels. In traditional filmmaking, special effects teams go to great lengths to make sure objects move and interact according to the laws of physics, whether it's a character walking through a room or a vehicle speeding down a road. AI models have struggled with this in the past, often producing awkward, unrealistic movements that break immersion. MovieGen, on the other hand, applies physics in a way that feels intuitive and natural.

Characters move fluidly, objects have weight and momentum, and scenes unfold with a sense of physical reality that rivals human-created content.

For example, in one of the demonstration videos, a man holding a fiery object in his hand performs wide, circular motions, all while standing barefoot on the shore with calm seas in the background. What's most impressive is how the AI captures the interplay of firelight with the man's body and the surrounding environment. The fire casts flickering shadows, the man's movements are smooth and synchronized with the flames, and the calm sea reflects the fire's glow in a way that feels astonishingly real. These are the types of details that make all the difference in creating immersive video content, and MovieGen handles them with ease.

While competitors like Runway Gen 3 and Sora have their strengths, MovieGen's ability to handle these complex elements of video creation puts it on a different level. Sora may generate visually appealing animations, but it struggles with fine details like lighting transitions or realistic physics. Runway Gen 3 offers dynamic visuals, but it often falls short when it comes to creating coherent, full-length videos that maintain quality from start to finish. MovieGen outshines them both, particularly in how it maintains consistency and realism throughout every scene.

What makes this even more remarkable is how accessible MovieGen makes high-quality video creation. Before, producing content at this level would require extensive teams of professionals: directors, cinematographers, lighting specialists, and post-production editors all working together. With MovieGen, much of that complexity is simplified. It's not about replacing human creativity but enhancing it, allowing creators to focus on their ideas while the AI handles the technical execution.

For content creators, marketers, and filmmakers, this marks the beginning of a new era. Imagine being able to describe a scene, down to the smallest detail, and watch it unfold before your eyes—realistic lighting, lifelike movement, and perfect physics all included. The creative possibilities are endless. Meta has, with MovieGen, not only joined the video AI race but leaped ahead, providing creators with a tool that not only matches but exceeds their expectations.

This technological breakthrough signals a shift in how we think about video creation. No longer constrained by the limits of human resources or the intricacies of post-production, creators are now free to dream bigger, to push the boundaries of storytelling further. The future of visual content isn't just about what can be captured by a camera—it's about what can be imagined and brought to life by AI. And with MovieGen, that future has never looked brighter.

Chapter 2: The Power of Text-to-Video

MovieGen represents a remarkable leap in artificial intelligence, particularly in the realm of text-to-video technology. Imagine being able to describe a scene, no matter how complex or vivid, and watching it come to life on screen with stunning detail. This is exactly what MovieGen does, transforming simple text prompts into high-quality videos that capture the nuances of the scenes described. It's a breakthrough that redefines creativity, opening up new possibilities for content creators, filmmakers, marketers, and storytellers.

With just a few lines of text, MovieGen can generate scenes that rival those produced by traditional production teams, eliminating the need for extensive physical resources.

At its core, the power of MovieGen lies in its ability to understand and process language at a deep level.

The system takes in text prompts and breaks them down into visual components, analyzing each part of the description to ensure that every detail is represented in the final video. Whether it's the setting, the characters, or the objects within the scene, MovieGen carefully interprets the input to ensure that what appears on screen closely matches the original vision. The result is a seamless blend of creativity and technology, where words are transformed into immersive, dynamic visuals.

One of the key strengths of MovieGen is its versatility. It's capable of handling a wide range of scenarios, from action-packed sequences to serene, meditative landscapes. A perfect example of this is the system's ability to generate something as visually complex as a fiery dance performance. In one demonstration, a user provided a simple text prompt: "A man holding a fiery object in his hand creates wide, circular motions, standing barefoot with a calm sea in the background." The resulting video was breathtaking, with the flames dancing in time with the man's movements, casting flickering shadows across his body and the surrounding environment. The calm sea in the background reflected the fiery glow, adding depth and realism to the scene. It's this kind of attention to detail that makes MovieGen stand out from other AI-generated video systems.

What's even more impressive is how MovieGen handles different lighting conditions and physical interactions. In the fiery dance video, for instance, the AI didn't just place a fire in the man's hand. It calculated how the light from the flames would interact with his skin, how it would reflect off the water, and how it would cast shadows on the ground.

These are the small yet critical details that take a scene from being just another AI-generated clip to something that feels genuinely lifelike. MovieGen's ability to simulate complex lighting conditions is one of its most powerful features, and it's a game-changer in creating immersive video content.

Beyond action-packed sequences, MovieGen also excels in creating more tranquil, serene scenes. In another demonstration, a user input a prompt describing a sloth floating on a donut-shaped pool float, sipping a tropical drink. The generated video captured the laid-back vibe perfectly, from the sunlight glinting off the water to the gentle sway of the sloth as it relaxed. What's truly impressive is how the AI managed to incorporate the small details that give the scene its charm.

For instance, the reflections of the water on the pool's surface were incredibly realistic, with ripples and light dancing around the float in a natural, believable way. Even the sloth's sunglasses cast subtle shadows, adding to the overall realism of the scene.

The ability to move seamlessly between different types of scenes, from high-energy action to slow, peaceful moments, demonstrates the incredible range of MovieGen's capabilities. It doesn't matter if the prompt describes a bustling city street or a quiet forest glade; MovieGen is able to adapt its approach to fit the tone and atmosphere of the scene. This flexibility is a major asset for creators, as it allows them to experiment with different ideas and visual styles without needing to switch between tools or systems. Everything is handled within the same platform, making the creative process smoother and more intuitive.

A critical aspect of what makes MovieGen's videos so engaging is its mastery of physics and dynamic lighting. These are areas where many

AI-generated video systems have traditionally struggled. Getting objects to move in a way that adheres to the laws of physics, or ensuring that lighting interacts naturally with the environment, can be extremely challenging.

However, MovieGen has developed sophisticated algorithms that allow it to overcome these hurdles. When objects move within a scene, they do so with a sense of weight and momentum that feels natural. Whether it's a person walking across a room or a car speeding down a street, the movements are fluid and realistic, giving the video a sense of authenticity.

In one particularly striking example, a video was generated showing a monkey bathing in a natural hot spring, playing with a miniature sailboat. The physics in this scene were handled with incredible accuracy. As the boat floated on the surface of the water, tiny ripples spread outward in response to the monkey's movements. The reflections of the boat and the surrounding greenery were also captured perfectly, with the lighting adjusting dynamically based on the position of the sun. This kind of realism is essential in creating videos that truly immerse the viewer, making them forget that what they're watching was generated by an AI.

Dynamic lighting plays a huge role in enhancing the immersion of AI-generated videos. In the past, AI systems often struggled with lighting, producing visuals that looked flat or unnatural. MovieGen, however, excels in this area, using advanced lighting models to simulate how light behaves in the real world. For example, in a video where a girl runs across a beach holding a kite, the AI accurately simulates how the sunlight hits the sand, creating shadows that follow the contours of her footsteps. As she runs, the sun reflects off the waves in the distance, adding a layer of depth to the scene.

This dynamic interaction between light and objects creates a sense of realism that draws the viewer in, making the video feel like something you could reach out and touch.

The impact of accurate physics and dynamic lighting on viewer immersion cannot be overstated. These are the elements that make a video feel real, even when it's entirely generated by an AI. Without them, the viewer is constantly reminded that what they're watching is artificial, breaking the suspension of disbelief. With MovieGen, however, the combination of lifelike physics and realistic lighting creates videos that are not only visually stunning but also deeply engaging. The viewer becomes absorbed in the scene, lost in the world that has been created, even if it's something as simple as a sloth floating on a pool float.

In conclusion, MovieGen's text-to-video capabilities represent a revolutionary shift in how we approach video creation. The ability to generate high-quality, immersive videos from a few lines of text is a game-changer for creators across all industries. From fiery dances to serene tropical scenes, MovieGen's mastery of physics, lighting, and visual detail sets a new standard for AI-generated content. The future of storytelling has arrived, and it's more dynamic, immersive, and accessible than ever before.

Chapter 3: Personalized Video Editing with AI

One of the most exciting aspects of MovieGen's capabilities lies in its personalized video editing features. While generating high-quality videos from simple text prompts is impressive on its own, Meta didn't stop there. They took the technology a step further by introducing post-training extensions that allow users to customize videos with incredible ease. These extensions are designed to give creators more control over the final product, making it possible to tweak and personalize videos without requiring any technical expertise.

This level of customization transforms MovieGen from a tool that generates content into one that truly empowers creators to mold and shape their vision.

At the heart of this innovation are MovieGen's post-training extensions, which allow for precise editing of the videos the AI generates.

Once a video is created, these extensions enable users to refine specific details, ensuring that every element of the video matches their desired outcome. What sets MovieGen apart from other AI video systems is the simplicity with which these adjustments can be made. Rather than diving into complicated software or requiring advanced knowledge of video editing tools, creators can make changes using nothing more than simple text inputs.

Imagine you've generated a beautiful scene with MovieGen—a man running through a desert, with the wind kicking up sand in his wake. The scene is visually stunning, but you want to add a few personal touches to give it a unique flavor. With MovieGen, you can easily modify the scene by typing in text-based instructions.

For instance, you could tell the system to add blue pom poms to the man's hands or change his outfit to an inflatable dinosaur costume. The AI takes care of the rest, seamlessly integrating these changes into the video without breaking the immersion or the overall flow of the scene.

One of the key strengths of this system is its ability to accurately interpret these text-based commands and reflect them in a way that feels natural within the video. Adding blue pom poms to a running man's hands might seem like a whimsical request, but MovieGen handles it with grace. Not only do the pom poms appear, but the AI also ensures that the physics of the scene are maintained. The pom poms move as they would if they were real, swaying with the motion of the man's hands and reacting to the wind in the environment.

It's these small, dynamic touches that elevate MovieGen's capabilities beyond simple video generation into the realm of true creative control.

Another striking example comes from a case where a user wanted to change the environment of an existing video. In the original clip, a man is seen running across a desert landscape. However, the user wanted to alter the setting to make it more playful and fun. With a simple text command, the desert was transformed into a carnival-like environment, complete with colorful tents and a vibrant backdrop. The AI didn't just replace the desert with random carnival elements; it carefully integrated them into the scene, ensuring that the lighting and shadows were consistent with the new environment. This level of attention to detail allows creators to modify their videos in a way that feels organic and seamless.

Costume changes are another area where MovieGen excels. In one demonstration, a user requested to replace a character's regular running outfit with an inflatable dinosaur costume. Not only did the costume appear exactly as instructed, but the AI also captured the unique way such a costume would behave in real life. The head of the inflatable dinosaur bobbed up and down in a humorous, yet realistic, manner as the character continued to run. This attention to physics and movement is crucial in maintaining the realism of the scene, even when fantastical elements are introduced.

MovieGen's ability to customize content goes beyond adding quirky elements or changing costumes. It allows creators to fundamentally alter the tone and atmosphere of a video. One particularly striking example involved a video where a girl was running along the beach, holding a kite. The original scene was bright and sunny, with a clear blue sky overhead. However, the user wanted to shift the mood of the video, requesting that the sky be changed to display the Northern Lights instead. MovieGen responded by transforming the bright daytime sky into a mesmerizing display of aurora borealis, bathing the entire scene in ethereal light. Despite the drastic change, the video retained its realism, with the lighting on the character and the environment shifting accordingly to match the new setting.

In addition to these visual changes, MovieGen also allows for alterations to the physical interactions within a scene. For example, in a video of a girl running on a sandy beach, the AI was able to accurately simulate the girl's footsteps in the sand. As her feet moved, the sand reacted in real-time, creating footprints that matched her stride. This level of physical detail is crucial in maintaining the viewer's suspension of disbelief. It's easy to overlook these subtle touches, but they play a significant role in making AI-generated content feel immersive and real.

One of the most intriguing aspects of MovieGen's customization features is how effortlessly they integrate into the existing video.

These aren't afterthoughts or separate overlays slapped on top of a video—they are woven into the fabric of the scene, interacting with the environment in a way that feels natural. When a user adds new objects, changes costumes, or alters the setting, the AI recalculates how the lighting, shadows, and physics should behave, ensuring that everything remains cohesive. This is what sets MovieGen apart as a personalized video editing tool.

The potential applications for this kind of customization are vast. For content creators, this means being able to fine-tune every aspect of their videos without needing to spend hours in complex editing software. For marketers and businesses, it means being able to quickly adapt content to suit different campaigns or audiences. And for filmmakers, it opens up a world of creative possibilities, where they can experiment with different versions of a scene until they achieve the perfect look and feel.

Meta's MovieGen isn't just an AI that generates videos; it's a tool that gives creators the power to personalize and perfect their content in ways that were previously unimaginable. By combining the ease of text-based input with the sophistication of its post-training extensions, MovieGen allows users to not only generate high-quality videos but also mold them to fit their unique vision. This is where the future of video editing is heading—toward a place where creativity isn't limited by the tools we use but enhanced by the possibilities they provide.

Chapter 4: Audio Innovation: MovieGen's 13 Billion Parameter Audio Model

One of the most significant advancements that MovieGen brings to the table is its ability to not only generate high-quality videos but also to seamlessly pair them with equally high-quality sound. Video is undoubtedly a powerful medium, but without the right audio, even the most visually stunning scenes can feel incomplete. MovieGen's audio model, powered by 13 billion parameters, takes care of this critical aspect by creating sound that perfectly matches the visuals it generates, bringing an additional layer of immersion to the experience.

This ability to generate cohesive, realistic audio sets MovieGen apart from many other

AI-driven video creation tools, which often struggle to create sound that feels truly integrated with the images on screen.

MovieGen's 13 billion parameter audio model works by analyzing the visual elements of a scene and generating sounds that match what's happening on screen. For instance, if the video shows a bustling marketplace, the audio might include the sounds of footsteps, distant chatter, vendors calling out, and the clatter of items being moved. If the scene involves a car chase, MovieGen can produce the roaring engines, screeching tires, and ambient city noises that would accompany such a sequence.

What's most impressive about this system is its ability to accurately generate both diegetic and nondiegetic sounds—an important distinction in the world of filmmaking and video production.

Diegetic sounds refer to those that originate from the world within the video. These are the sounds that the characters in the scene can hear, such as dialogue, footsteps, or the rustling of leaves.

Non-diegetic sounds, on the other hand, are those that exist outside the world of the video, often used to enhance the mood or provide additional context. Examples include background music, a narrator's voice, or sound effects added for dramatic effect, like the suspenseful music during a tense moment. MovieGen's audio model is adept at generating both types of sounds, ensuring that they complement the visuals without feeling out of place or jarring.

For example, in a scene where a man is performing a fiery dance on a beach, MovieGen doesn't just create the sound of the fire crackling—it also generates the ambient sounds of the ocean waves in the background and the wind blowing gently across the sand. These sounds are diegetic, as they are a natural part of the environment that the character would also be experiencing.

What's remarkable about MovieGen's audio model is how it handles these subtle elements. The sound of the waves isn't overbearing or out of sync with the visuals; instead, it ebbs and flows in harmony with the movement of the water on screen. Similarly, the crackling of the fire adjusts in volume and intensity depending on the proximity of the flames to the camera, creating a dynamic audio experience that mirrors the visuals perfectly.

MovieGen's ability to generate non-diegetic sounds is equally impressive. In many cases, non-diegetic audio is used to heighten the emotional impact of a scene, and MovieGen has been trained to understand these emotional cues. In the same beach scene, for instance, the AI might add a soft, melancholic musical score in the background, designed to evoke a specific feeling in the viewer. This music wouldn't be part of the actual world within the video—the character wouldn't hear it—but it would serve to guide the audience's emotional response. MovieGen's audio model is capable of crafting music and soundscapes that align with the tone of the visuals, enhancing the overall storytelling experience.

One of the standout examples of MovieGen's audio capabilities comes from a video it generated of a sloth lounging on a donut-shaped pool float, sipping a tropical drink. The visuals alone are charming, but it's the audio that truly brings the scene to life. The AI generated the gentle lapping of the pool water against the float, the occasional rustle of palm trees swaying in the breeze, and the distant sound of birds chirping in the background.

These diegetic sounds create a sense of place, transporting the viewer to this tropical paradise. But MovieGen didn't stop there—it also added a non-diegetic layer, with soft, relaxing music that perfectly complements the laid-back atmosphere of the scene. The result is an immersive experience that feels both visually and sonically cohesive.

The precision with which MovieGen generates audio extends to more complex scenes as well. In a case where a video shows a monkey playing in a natural hot spring, the AI doesn't simply overlay generic water sounds. Instead, it accurately captures the sound of the monkey splashing in the water, the quiet hum of insects in the surrounding foliage, and the faint echo of the monkey's movements reverberating off the rocks around the spring.

These diegetic sounds are so carefully crafted that they feel almost as if they were recorded on set, adding a layer of authenticity that is often missing in AI-generated content.

Furthermore, the non-diegetic elements in this scene, such as the serene background music, serve to enhance the tranquil mood. The sound doesn't overpower the natural environment but instead blends in, making the scene feel more like a complete sensory experience. This balance between diegetic and nondiegetic sound is one of MovieGen's greatest strengths. It doesn't just generate audio; it understands how to use sound to tell a story, ensuring that every noise, every note, plays a role in bringing the scene to life.

MovieGen's ability to produce long, coherent audio tracks for videos that span several minutes is another feature that sets it apart. Many AI systems struggle with maintaining consistent audio quality over extended periods, often resulting in loops or repetitive soundscapes that break immersion.

However, MovieGen's audio model has been fine-tuned to generate audio that evolves naturally over time.

This is especially important in scenes with a lot of action or environmental changes. For instance, in a video where a girl is running along a beach, the sound of her footsteps in the sand would change as she moves from wet, packed sand near the water to softer, dry sand farther from the shore. The AI recognizes these changes and adjusts the sound accordingly, keeping the audio consistent with the evolving visuals.

The audio generated by MovieGen isn't just high-quality in terms of content—it's also produced at a professional standard. The AI is capable of generating sound at 48 kHz, which is the standard for cinematic audio. This ensures that the audio is clear, crisp, and suitable for use in professional media projects, whether they be films, games, or marketing videos. The fact that MovieGen can achieve this level of audio quality automatically, without the need for manual sound engineering, is a testament to the sophistication of Meta's AI technology.

In summary, MovieGen's 13 billion parameter audio model is a game-changer in video production. Its ability to generate both diegetic and nondiegetic sounds that perfectly match the visuals elevates the overall storytelling experience, making AI-generated videos feel more immersive and polished than ever before. From the subtle rustling of leaves to the crescendo of a cinematic score, MovieGen ensures that every sound plays a role in crafting a complete, engaging narrative.

Whether it's the clink of a glass in a tropical scene or the roar of an engine in a fast-paced car chase, MovieGen's audio capabilities ensure that what you hear is just as compelling as what you see.

Chapter 5: Breaking Down Key Use Cases

MovieGen's potential to revolutionize the world of professional filmmaking and content creation is undeniable. As AI becomes more integrated into the creative process, the boundaries of what can be achieved are constantly expanding. Meta's MovieGen is leading this charge by providing creators with a powerful tool that goes beyond generating simple, pre-programmed visuals. It is capable of producing high-quality, dynamic videos based on text prompts, allowing filmmakers and content creators to push the limits of their imagination with minimal technical effort.

By breaking down the key use cases of MovieGen, it becomes clear that its impact will stretch far beyond today's practices, offering a glimpse into a future where AI is at the heart of visual storytelling.

One of the most immediate and obvious applications for MovieGen is in professional filmmaking. Traditionally, creating a high-quality film requires a vast array of resources—actors, directors, cinematographers, lighting experts, sound engineers, and countless others, all working in harmony to bring a vision to life. Every shot requires meticulous planning, and post-production can take months or even years to perfect.

MovieGen streamlines this process by eliminating many of the labor-intensive tasks associated with filmmaking. With its ability to generate entire scenes from simple text inputs, filmmakers can now focus on the creative aspects of their work, leaving much of the technical heavy lifting to the AI.

Imagine a filmmaker wants to create a scene set in a futuristic city, complete with towering skyscrapers, flying vehicles, and crowds of people.

Instead of scouting locations, hiring extras, or spending months on visual effects, the filmmaker could simply describe the scene to MovieGen. The AI would then generate a highly detailed, visually stunning video that matches the prompt, complete with realistic lighting, shadows, and physics. This not only saves time and resources but also opens the door to creative possibilities that were once limited by budget or logistical constraints. The technology democratizes filmmaking, allowing even small studios or independent creators to produce content that rivals Hollywood blockbusters in terms of visual quality.

Beyond traditional filmmaking, MovieGen also holds immense potential in the world of content creation. As the demand for video content continues to grow across platforms like YouTube, TikTok, Instagram, and beyond, creators are constantly looking for ways to set themselves apart.

With MovieGen, these creators can produce unique, eye-catching content without needing extensive video editing skills. For instance, a YouTuber could use MovieGen to generate custom intros, animated sequences, or entire videos that align perfectly with their brand's aesthetic. The AI takes care of the complex tasks, freeing creators to focus on their message and audience engagement.

Moreover, MovieGen's ability to generate personalized videos allows content creators to tailor their videos to specific audiences. This could be particularly useful in marketing and advertising, where personalization has become a key strategy. A brand could, for example, create multiple versions of a video ad, each one customized to appeal to different demographics or regions, all without needing to film the ad multiple times. This level of customization has the potential to drastically improve the efficiency of marketing campaigns, making them more engaging and effective.

The implications for video editors are equally profound. Traditionally, video editing is a painstaking process that requires hours of detailed work. Editors must carefully cut, trim, and arrange footage, ensuring that every frame flows smoothly. With MovieGen, much of this manual labor is removed from the equation. The AI can generate and edit entire sequences based on simple text commands, adjusting lighting, adding special effects, or altering the physical interactions in a scene with ease.

This doesn't mean that editors are replaced by AI; rather, it allows them to focus on higher-level creative decisions while MovieGen handles the more technical aspects of the process. It's a powerful collaboration between human ingenuity and artificial intelligence, designed to make the editing process faster and more intuitive.

But the true potential of MovieGen lies in its future applications. As AI-generated content continues to evolve, the lines between human and machine-created art are becoming increasingly blurred. We're entering a future where filmmakers, content creators, and even everyday users can harness the power of AI to create professional-grade videos with unprecedented ease. For example, imagine a future where aspiring filmmakers, who previously lacked access to the expensive equipment and resources needed to make movies, can now bring their ideas to life using MovieGen.

This technology could foster a new wave of creativity, democratizing filmmaking and giving a voice to creators from all walks of life.

This also means that the entertainment industry could be on the verge of a major transformation.

Movie studios and production companies will be able to streamline their workflows, producing content faster and more efficiently than ever before. AI-generated content will likely become an integral part of the filmmaking process, not as a replacement for human creativity but as a tool that enhances it. Directors and producers will have access to an infinite range of visual possibilities, allowing them to experiment with different concepts, styles, and effects at a fraction of the cost and time it would take using traditional methods.

Additionally, as virtual reality and augmented reality continue to grow in popularity, AI-generated content like that produced by MovieGen could play a crucial role in developing immersive experiences. Imagine a fully interactive VR experience where users can shape the world around them simply by describing what they want to see. MovieGen could generate entire virtual environments in real time, adapting to the user's preferences and creating a truly personalized, immersive experience. This could revolutionize not only entertainment but also industries like education, training, and gaming.

For the entertainment industry as a whole, the introduction of AI-generated content could lead to a surge in innovation. Movie studios could use AI to experiment with new storytelling techniques, blending real and virtual elements in ways that were previously unimaginable. Independent filmmakers could use MovieGen to create films that rival big-budget productions in visual quality, all while working with a fraction of the resources.

And content creators, influencers, and marketers could take their videos to the next level, producing personalized, dynamic content that captures the attention of their audiences.

As AI continues to evolve, it's clear that the role of human creativity will remain essential. While AI like MovieGen can generate stunning visuals and perfectly synchronized audio, it is the human touch—the storytelling, the emotional connection, the artistic vision—that gives content its soul. MovieGen and similar AI tools will serve as enablers, empowering creators to dream bigger, work faster, and reach new heights in their creative endeavors.

In summary, the key use cases of MovieGen demonstrate its potential to reshape the landscape of filmmaking, content creation, and beyond. Its ability to generate high-quality, personalized video content opens up a world of possibilities for creators across all industries. The future implications for video editors, marketers, and filmmakers are immense, as AI-generated content begins to play an increasingly prominent role in the entertainment industry. As we look ahead, one thing is clear: MovieGen is not just a tool for today, but a glimpse into the future of visual storytelling.

Chapter 6: The Future of Dynamic Editing

As technology continues to evolve, the future of video editing is rapidly moving toward real-time customization, and MovieGen is at the forefront of this transformation. In an industry where the process of video creation has traditionally been time-consuming and resource-intensive, the ability to make dynamic, real-time edits marks a major breakthrough. With MovieGen, creators are no longer constrained by lengthy post-production processes or the need for specialized software.

Instead, they can adjust scenes on the fly, making rapid changes to everything from physics and lighting to character movements and environments, all through simple text-based commands. This level of control and immediacy represents the future of dynamic video editing, enabling creators to push the boundaries of what's possible in video production.

One of the most revolutionary aspects of MovieGen is its ability to respond to real-time inputs. This goes beyond the initial video generation based on text prompts. Once a video is created, users can continue to make changes, fine-tuning the details of the scene with additional prompts. Want to change the time of day in a scene? Simply input a command, and MovieGen will adjust the lighting to match. Want to swap out a character's outfit or introduce new elements into the background?

No problem—MovieGen can handle it all with a level of speed and precision that would have been unthinkable just a few years ago. The AI isn't just editing pre-existing footage; it's dynamically regenerating the scene based on the new information, ensuring that the changes feel organic and cohesive.

This real-time customization is particularly powerful when it comes to adjusting physics and lighting.

In traditional video production, simulating realistic physics—such as the way objects move, how they interact with their environment, or how light behaves in different settings—requires extensive time and expertise. These elements often need to be fine-tuned frame by frame, especially in special effects-heavy scenes. MovieGen simplifies this process by allowing users to make real-time adjustments that account for complex physical interactions and lighting dynamics without requiring deep technical knowledge.

For instance, imagine a scene where a character is running through a forest. The user may decide halfway through that they want to add a light rain to the environment. With traditional methods, this would require additional effects work, potentially reshooting or adjusting the lighting setup to ensure consistency.

With MovieGen, the user can simply input a prompt like "add light rain," and the system will instantly generate the appropriate environmental changes. The AI adjusts the lighting, accounting for the overcast skies that accompany the rain, and ensures that the raindrops interact naturally with the character's movements. The shadows shift, the reflections in the puddles are updated in real-time, and the entire scene is transformed without any additional manual editing.

This dynamic ability to adjust lighting in real-time is one of MovieGen's most impressive features. Lighting is often what gives a scene its emotional tone, influencing how the viewer feels and experiences the narrative. Whether it's the soft glow of a sunset or the harsh glare of artificial lighting, the way light interacts with the characters and setting is crucial for storytelling. With MovieGen, adjusting the lighting isn't a painstaking process—it's as simple as describing the desired effect. Whether you want to switch from a bright, sunny day to a moody, shadowy night scene, the AI understands how to reconfigure the entire video to match, changing the direction of shadows, the intensity of the light, and even how reflective surfaces behave under the new conditions.

Beyond the creative implications, this level of real-time customization holds significant potential for industries beyond entertainment. While the obvious application is in filmmaking, where directors and editors can now iterate rapidly on scenes, the technology extends to sectors like marketing, education, and virtual reality. For marketers, MovieGen's real-time capabilities mean that ads can be customized on the fly to suit different audiences or geographic regions, without needing to go through the lengthy process of creating entirely new content. For example, a company could produce a single ad, then use MovieGen to alter the background, product placement, or messaging to appeal to different demographics in real-time. This would drastically reduce production costs and allow for more tailored and effective campaigns.

In education, MovieGen's ability to dynamically edit videos in real-time could open up new possibilities for interactive learning. Imagine educational videos that can change based on a student's input or the needs of a specific lesson. A teacher could adjust a pre-existing video lesson to include more examples, change the visual focus, or highlight key points based on real-time classroom interaction.

This could lead to more engaging and personalized educational content, providing students with experiences that adapt to their learning pace and style.

Virtual reality (VR) and augmented reality (AR) are perhaps the most exciting areas where MovieGen's dynamic editing capabilities could make a major impact. In the world of VR and AR, the ability to make real-time changes to environments is essential for creating immersive experiences. MovieGen's AI could allow users to customize their virtual worlds instantly, altering everything from the layout of a virtual space to the weather conditions or time of day.

Imagine a VR environment where users can describe what they want to see, and MovieGen instantly reshapes the landscape to match their vision. This level of interaction could revolutionize how we engage with virtual spaces, whether for gaming, training simulations, or social interactions in digital worlds.

For industries like architecture and real estate, MovieGen's dynamic editing features could be used to create virtual walkthroughs of properties that adjust based on client preferences.

Want to see what a building would look like with different lighting or furniture arrangements? With MovieGen, these changes could be made in real-time, giving clients a more interactive and engaging way to explore properties before they're even built. This could significantly enhance the decision-making process in real estate and construction, providing a level of visualization that's both practical and innovative.

In live events or virtual presentations, the ability to edit visuals in real-time has enormous potential. Imagine a virtual conference where presenters can adjust their backgrounds or on-screen elements based on audience feedback, or a concert where the visuals evolve dynamically in response to the music or crowd energy. MovieGen's real-time editing capabilities could transform how we experience live events, blending digital and physical experiences into something entirely new.

In the broader context of video production, MovieGen's capabilities represent a paradigm shift. Historically, video editing has been a time-consuming process that required technical expertise and significant resources. With MovieGen, much of that process is streamlined, making video production faster, more flexible, and more accessible to creators of all skill levels. Whether it's tweaking the lighting on a film set, adding new elements to a virtual world, or customizing marketing content on the fly, MovieGen's real-time customization allows for unprecedented creative freedom.

Looking ahead, the potential applications of dynamic video editing extend far beyond what we see today. As AI continues to improve, we can expect even more sophisticated real-time editing features, where the boundaries between virtual and physical realities become increasingly blurred. The ability to edit videos on the fly, with AI that understands context, physics, and lighting, is poised to transform industries that rely on visual storytelling, allowing for more immersive, engaging, and personalized experiences across the board.

In conclusion, the future of dynamic editing is bright, with MovieGen at the helm. Its real-time video customization capabilities offer creators, marketers, educators, and innovators a powerful tool to shape their visual content with unparalleled ease and precision. By adjusting physics and lighting based on real-time inputs, MovieGen is revolutionizing not just how videos are made, but how we interact with them.

This technology opens up a world of possibilities, transforming video production across industries and redefining the role of AI in creative processes.

Chapter 7: Beyond the Screen: How AI is Reshaping Creativity

As artificial intelligence continues to evolve, its influence is extending far beyond the technical realms it once dominated. Now, AI is reshaping creativity itself, offering new tools, techniques, and opportunities to artists, filmmakers, marketers, designers, and content creators. In industries where human imagination has traditionally been the sole driver, AI is becoming a powerful collaborator.

The result is a new age of creativity where personalization, efficiency, and limitless possibilities intersect, allowing creators to push boundaries like never before. Among the many groundbreaking AI systems leading this charge, Meta's MovieGen stands out as a prime example of how AI can revolutionize visual content creation, blurring the lines between human ingenuity and machine intelligence.

The implications of AI in creative industries are vast and profound. In the past, creating visual content required immense resources—both human and technical. A single video might involve teams of experts, including directors, animators, sound engineers, and editors, all working in unison to bring an idea to life. This process could take weeks, months, or even years, depending on the complexity of the project. But with the advent of AI like MovieGen, much of the labor-intensive work involved in content creation is now streamlined or automated, freeing up human creators to focus on the heart of their work: storytelling, emotional resonance, and innovation.

One of the most significant advantages AI brings to the creative process is personalization. Today's consumers expect content that feels tailor-made for them. Whether it's a personalized marketing campaign, a product demo, or an immersive video experience, people are drawn to content that speaks directly to their needs, interests, and emotions.

AI makes this possible on a scale that was previously unimaginable. With tools like MovieGen, creators can generate multiple versions of the same content, each one customized for different audiences, demographics, or cultural contexts. This personalization can be done in real-time, allowing for dynamic, responsive content that adapts to the viewer's preferences.

For example, a brand might use MovieGen to create a marketing video for a global campaign. In the past, this would require producing separate videos for different regions, each with localized visuals, messaging, and cultural references. With MovieGen, the process becomes much simpler. The AI can generate a base video and then modify elements like background, characters, or product placement based on the target audience, all through text prompts. This level of efficiency allows brands to connect with diverse audiences in a more meaningful way, while drastically reducing production time and costs.

Efficiency is another critical factor where AI is reshaping the creative landscape. What once took days or weeks to achieve can now be accomplished in hours, if not minutes. MovieGen's ability to generate high-quality videos from simple text prompts cuts down the need for extensive pre-production work, scouting locations, or lengthy post-production edits. For independent filmmakers or small creative teams, this opens up possibilities that were previously out of reach.

A single creator with a vision can now produce content that rivals large studios, all thanks to the power of AI.

Moreover, AI like MovieGen is helping to democratize creativity. In the past, access to professional-grade tools and technology was limited to those with significant financial backing or technical expertise. Now, with AI-driven platforms, anyone with an idea can bring it to life. Whether it's a short film, a marketing campaign, or an artistic project, AI provides the means to create without the usual barriers of entry. This democratization is fostering a new wave of creativity, where voices that might have once been silenced by a lack of resources can now be heard.

One of the most exciting aspects of AI in creative industries is the potential for limitless creativity. Human imagination is boundless, but it has always been constrained by the tools available. With AI, those constraints are rapidly disappearing. MovieGen, for instance, allows creators to visualize scenes that might otherwise be impossible to produce in the real world. A filmmaker can describe a futuristic cityscape, a fantastical creature, or a dreamlike sequence, and MovieGen will bring it to life with stunning accuracy. This level of creative freedom empowers storytellers to explore new genres, styles, and narratives without the typical limitations of budget, time, or technology.

In addition, AI is enabling creators to experiment more freely. In the traditional creative process, trying out different ideas often meant investing significant time and resources, with no guarantee that the result would be successful. With MovieGen, creators can rapidly prototype different versions of a scene, a video, or even an entire narrative, tweaking elements like lighting, tone, or character design until they achieve the desired effect.

This ability to iterate quickly and easily fosters a more exploratory approach to creativity, where failure is no longer costly but an integral part of the creative journey.

Beyond the immediate benefits of personalization, efficiency, and creative freedom, AI is also reshaping the role of human creators. Rather than replacing human creativity, AI acts as an extension of it, amplifying what humans can achieve. With tools like MovieGen handling the technical aspects of content creation—such as physics simulations, lighting adjustments, and sound synchronization—creators can focus on what they do best: crafting compelling stories, evoking emotions, and connecting with their audiences on a deeper level.

This collaboration between human creativity and machine intelligence is where the true potential of AI lies. Instead of viewing AI as a competitor, creators are beginning to see it as a partner, one that can take care of the repetitive, time-consuming tasks, leaving more room for artistic vision and innovation. In the same way that past technological advancements—such as the camera, the printing press, or the internet—expanded the horizons of creative expression, AI is now offering a new set of tools that can enhance, rather than diminish, the creative process.

MovieGen, as part of this AI revolution, exemplifies the intersection of art and technology. By seamlessly blending visual storytelling with advanced AI capabilities, it empowers creators to realize their visions in ways that were once unimaginable. Whether it's generating realistic environments, dynamically adjusting scenes in real-time, or customizing content for specific audiences, MovieGen represents a fundamental shift in how visual content is produced and consumed.

Looking ahead, the role of AI in creative industries will only continue to grow. As AI becomes more sophisticated, its ability to understand and respond to human input will improve, leading to even more intuitive and powerful creative tools. This opens up exciting possibilities for the future of entertainment, art, marketing, and beyond. We may see new forms of interactive media, where AI-generated content evolves in response to audience input, or entirely new genres of film and storytelling that emerge from the unique capabilities of AI.

In conclusion, the broader implications of AI in creative industries are transformative. With tools like MovieGen, creators can now personalize content with unprecedented ease, produce high-quality visuals at a fraction of the time and cost, and explore creative possibilities that were once beyond reach. The potential for limitless creativity is no longer a distant dream but a reality that is reshaping the future of visual storytelling.

MovieGen stands as a testament to AI's role in this revolution, offering a glimpse into the new era of creativity that is unfolding before our eyes.

CONCLUSION

As we reach the conclusion of this journey through the remarkable innovations of MovieGen, it's clear that we are standing at the precipice of a new era in visual storytelling. What was once confined to the realms of imagination and technical complexity has now been made accessible, thanks to Meta's groundbreaking AI. From generating entire scenes through simple text prompts to dynamically editing videos in real-time, MovieGen is not just a tool but a gateway to limitless creative possibilities. It has redefined how we approach filmmaking, content creation, and artistic expression.

The implications of AI-driven video creation go beyond convenience or efficiency—they represent a fundamental shift in how we understand and utilize technology in creative industries. MovieGen's ability to personalize content, automate complex processes, and enhance storytelling has empowered creators across all sectors to elevate their work. Whether it's a filmmaker experimenting with new narratives, a content creator producing personalized videos, or a marketer targeting diverse audiences, MovieGen has made it easier than ever to translate ideas into reality.

But the true power of this technology lies not in the automation of tasks but in its ability to enhance human creativity. AI doesn't replace the creative spark—it amplifies it. With AI handling the technical details, creators are free to focus on what truly matters: the emotions, ideas, and stories that connect us all. By removing the barriers of time, resources, and technical expertise, AI like MovieGen opens the door to more voices, more visions, and more stories than ever before.

As we look to the future, it's exciting to imagine how AI will continue to evolve and shape the creative landscape. From virtual reality experiences to interactive media and beyond, the possibilities are endless. MovieGen represents a crucial step forward in this journey, demonstrating what's possible when cutting-edge technology is placed in the hands of creators. It's a tool that is already changing the way we produce and consume visual content, and it promises to play a pivotal role in the future of entertainment, education, marketing, and more.

In this ever-changing landscape, one thing remains constant: the human desire to tell stories. MovieGen is a powerful tool that enhances this timeless pursuit, allowing us to push the boundaries of what we can imagine and create. As AI continues to reshape the world of creativity, it is not replacing the artist but giving them new mediums through which to express their vision.

The future of visual storytelling has never been more exciting, and with tools like MovieGen, we are only just beginning to scratch the surface of what's possible.

In closing, MovieGen stands as a testament to the power of AI in reshaping not just how we create, but how we think about creativity itself. It offers a glimpse into a future where imagination is truly unlimited, where the only boundaries are those we choose to set for ourselves. Whether you are an aspiring filmmaker, an artist, a content creator, or simply someone with a story to tell, MovieGen offers the tools to make that story come to life in ways you've never imagined before. The future of creativity is here—and it's being shaped by AI.